TRICKSTER

KUHL HOUSE POETS

edited by Mark Levine and Emily Wilson

TRICKSTER

poems by RANDALL POTTS

UNIVERSITY OF IOWA PRESS

IOWA CITY

University of Iowa Press, Iowa City 52242
Copyright © 2014 by Randall Potts
www.uiowapress.org
Printed in the United States of America

Design by Barbara Haines

The University of Iowa Press is a member of Green Press Initiative
and is committed to preserving natural resources.

Printed on acid-free paper

ISBN: 978-1-60938-284-1 (pbk)
ISBN: 978-1-60938-295-7 (ebk)
LCCN: 2014935649

For Robin, John, Geoff, & S.

CONTENTS

I

"I was not created for this, but I did this . . ."

—*Wakdjunkaga*

Trickster

The more I struggle
The worse it gets.
I buy a coat, then
I'm too thin to wear it.
I buy a house, then
Wind covers it in smoke.
I make a garden, then
Wind covers it in smoke.
I sit in my house coughing.
I write a poem, then
You assume my poem
Is about you, then
You hate my poem.
"You're a liar," you say.
How was I to know
You were thin, your garden
Was covered in smoke
That you sat in your house
Coughing?

Nest

Sun drops behind the Magnolia & I see
the Yellow Jacket's nest, hung like a horn-of-plenty
under the wide leaves—a thread of Wasps spooling
out its dark hole mumbling threats—
a corner of the garden that's no longer ours.

The man who's come to kill Wasps wants to save them—
"it's just summer & fall," he says, "then the Queen dies
& things break down, a fall freeze kills the rest . . .
a new Queen hides in a woodpile or under the bark
of a tree, 'til the summer heat rouses her—"
but *what's the end?* I want to know.

"It's just one Queen begets a nest," says the man come
to kill Wasps—but I'm already dreaming (of angels
& a ranch house far down the coast)
a boy who puts his head through windows (& a din
that won't stop shouting), an old woman
with her suitcase by the door, threatening & threatened—
now he's losing his nerve, this man who kills Wasps
I have to tell him again, "yes, kill them."

A Natural History

1.

Salmon, farmed & wild, lie gill-to-gill
sliced open on white butcher shop ice—
wild twice the size of farmed, one white
the other a deep orange—"it's Shellfish
they feed on makes them orange"
the Butcher says, shrugging his shoulders
"the wild ones, they eat whatever they want"
everything passing through everything else
(no one shape left alone) always food & self.
He points to a seam along the silver scales
"every Fish has one," he says
"a way in—"

2.

"When I was little," the woman said
as we stood by the bonfire, our backs to the Woods
"the Butcher would come in his white panel truck
& he & my father go down to the barn . . .
I led in a Goat, so the Sheep would follow—
hid behind the door as my father swung
a metal pole, crushed the Sheep's skull—
They butchered it there in the hay, piled it
in a wheelbarrow, balanced the head on top:
'Take it up to the house, don't spill it' he said . . .
I lifted the handles & the head rolled free, bounced
in the hay—what could I do? but pick it up
by its soft ears, balance it on the bloody bits
& go on?"

The Good Life

1.
Pines twist in a spring gale.
I dig weeds before they flower & spread
Spook pink Worms, am friend to Robins

Plainspoken trees
& leafless brambles can't confuse:
I lime the lawn to feed grass, kill the moss

sure of my allegiances—
shade for Orange Cat, seeds for Chickadees . . .
light losing its dull grief

Ravens traveling two-by-two.

2.
I take a hacksaw to the Laurel, make visible
a path—this was our plan, after all, I must
prune the garden of uselessness, guilty

you must burn the sausages, this was our plan
to break siege, the slow attrition
to put our profits in the future—

this sliver of land, our grass alive
with newborn Spiders, Night Crawlers
that retreat into themselves—

I crank a wave of seeds
dirt under my nails, your hands washing mine
before we fled.

The Ranch

It's the first day
of Deer hunting season—
a red truck waits by the gate, its patience
inexhaustible, its men still out
in the heat . . . no shots fired
so, it's still hypothetical
like the Pig or what remained
of the Pig, rotten, emptied from the freezer
was hypothetical—
until Coyotes yelped all night
& tore it to bits.

I sleep past you
afraid of what we'll find—
a day already limping away
"Just wing it," you say, while
at the feeder, Hummingbirds slash & parry
while 4-H kids try to sell us the animals
they've raised, the Sheep & Swine
named, tamed, fattened for prize
& love—you can't help but pity them
when they say, "I spent the winter
with my Sheep . . ."

Smoke from a fire
up north turns the sky feverish—
I can't work the radio, neither can you
so we wait: "the Dane's a palace dog"
you say, "bred to inspire, you can't help but try

to please him" & his master, groaning
his way to sleep (further even than sleep)
lost in the body he destroyed, he
is the one we wait for, lunging
for the leather chair, (a halo of grease
where his head lay) a Scotch
held like a torch as the air parts before him—
"I'm just trying to be useful," I say
"Useful's most misunderstood"
he says, "some's ruined their lives for
useful," he says, as the air
parts before him—

Red-winged Black-
birds' scolding chatter draws
it out—the heat agrees, we have turned
our backs to the future & we wait—
the horse called Sarah who had to be shot
has been shot & skinned & left to
the Vultures, her legs & head still whole
her body just a bloody curve of ribs
& pelvis, her eyes gone, her teeth bared
& still we wait—

Day ripens away
from us—"it's too soon" you say
we suck the bitter from the grapes
spit them in the orange dust—
a Hawk drops out of the blue, Blackbirds scatter
& it's quiet for the first time in days
(I notice the bones in your face)

call it mercy—everything else
argues against us: a night made sleepless by heat
the shotgun, breech open (two greasy holes)
for rage that cannot find its way to grief—
the road is (all blind curves)
one black lane, tunneling out
the chaparral.

Stalker

—for A. Tarkovsky

Here, in the meat grinder
Squirrels click their teeth, fear
in their black eyes—

wide-bladed Weeds open
cracks in flagstone, a bushy green
right to the rickety steps & I—

I'm this afternoon, all life long:

a warm spell tricks Aphids
into hatching, one momentarily golden
flutters, then goes gray—

a boy with a stick swings at it—

they say "the wild Onion's musk
rhymes its girlish flowers," but it won't
& neither will you, neither will I—

Hawk rips open a Robin
the desperate flock drives him
from the Oak—

Hawk, phalanx of Robins—

ask the Worm, ask
the Cat, ask the Dove
ask—

"my face sharpens away to bone
your face sharpens away
to bone—"

Passport

I oscillate—
Ideas like leaves, color
Drift off, lost—

I cry out, "Who
In the green world?—"
Helplessly. Panic—

I am not rooted—
Yet my body tethered
Yet my mind

Hinged upon
All the green world—
So, I am rooted.

Who can deny it?

The Inquisitor

The Inquisitor is pleased—
My lover is a wooden doll floating, passing
Face down, irretrievable—
"Your fault," She says, "all your fault."

My lover is a wooden doll floating, passing
Like the slow eclipse of a bloodied Moon—
"Your fault," She says, "all your fault."
My always failing self, again failing

Like the slow eclipse of a bloodied Moon—
Maples stripped of their yellow & red
My always failing self, again failing
To let the real be real.

Maples stripped of their yellow & red
Leaves like lanterns light the path—
To let the real be real.
If I agree, who am I? Who's She?

Leaves like lanterns light the path—
The Inquisitor is pleased—
If I agree, who am I? Who's She?
Face down, irretrievable—

Balance

I can't go on as I am.
I keep falling.
I'll doctor me.
I'll agree on words.
I'll make pictures of questions.
By then, it'll be dark.
I'll send ears on ahead.
No one will surprise us.
I'll pull shadow from elbow.
I'll bury me in night.

Dream

No color.

I'm black & white.

Bees hum their gold.

They swarm.

I kneel in grass.

I try to be small.

I feel Bees on me.

Too many Bees

Walking on me.

A boy yells, "He's

Being stung—"

But I'm not stung.

My eyes open.

Dream

I dream a reactor to ruin
A dam to rubble—

"Someday machines
Can finish your work," I shout
To the Watchmen—

To dark city hills I sing:
"Sleep, sleep
Let us vanish without trace!"

To myself I whisper, "*My body is a fuse
I have begun to burn.*"

Undoing

Big Fly keeps at me.
No one lets me alone.
I look for a place
To plunge my hand in
To pull a curse out—
To set hills Walking.

I'm closing in.
I climb in creek bed
To follow roots—
Make a ring of sand
Balance my forefinger
& forget where I am.

Ground sends a route
Straight up my arm—
That sets me Walking.

Walk

1.

Wind pile
Nest bowl
Things-happen
Web-droplets
Aster star
Holes

2.

Fog
Antlers
Pollen maze
Bee-hum
Footprints
Herd-walking
Dust spirals
Tunnels
Salt

3.

Greasy light
Grass rattle
Oak-leaves-click
True-name
Heaviness
Forest eyes
Raven-walking
Spit

4.
Cicada

II

"He sang on like a harmful bird."

—*John Berryman*

Fable

I go poorly.
Cold says, "let me nibble your feet."
"No," I say.

"Only your toes, let me nibble them," says Cold.
"No," I say.

Cold says, "let me nibble your hands."
"No," I say.

"Only your fingertips, let me nibble them," says Cold, "just a little bit."
"No," I say.

Frost smears the grass.

"I'm hungry," says Cold.
I say nothing.

"Let me nibble your ears," says Cold.
"No," I say.

Oak leaves tick, tick.

"Let me nibble your nose, only the tip of your nose," says Cold.
"Only the tip? OK," I say.

"Good," says Cold.
The tip of my nose is cold, too cold.

Cold is hungry and can't stop—
"Stop!" I shout. But it's too late.
I'm Cold.

Folklore

1. Feral

"What are we talking about?"
I ask Wind, "What are we
Talking about?" I ask Tree—

"You must stop talking!"
Says Stone, "I can't hear Myself
Think; you're too noisy—"

So I lay on Stone's belly
And Stone warmed me.

2. Trailhead

Spring grass trail
Only a couple of inches wide
Swerving to Coyote Brush—

Rabbit? Weasel? I can't
Read this passage in language
I was never taught.

So, at creek bed, listen:
Water teaches us a song—
What are we humming?

3. Dusk Chorus

Alders insist on drinking first
I'm pale & skinny like them

Coyote's light-footed
Shadow dissolves in tasseled grass—

A Red-winged Blackbird keens—
A Gopher leans out

Pulls down a weed:
He's chewing—

Swarm

1000s of Lady Bugs swarm
Over meadow's percolating heat.

Sunlight glints on their flickering wings
Breeze swirls & billows them

They jitter, shape-shift in the light
On their auspicious spring awakening—

As I stride through a square knot
Not a wing touches me, they compensate

Like a song of bright orange notes
They improvise their twirling melody—

To me a song as airy as sleep—
Before the dirge

Of Summer.

Divide Meadow

Forest unhooks me—
At "Divide Meadow" I can't divide:
One insists.

Big Fly talks me out, fills me in:

Meadow is many
Smeared with life, black Spiders
Tending their nets—

Letting One exist.

Metamorphosis

One woman becomes the wind that holds her.
Another falls helplessly onto yellow.
Two women run on a beach, ecstatic: they are alive.
Their hair trails into clouds, becomes clouds.
They rush on, their hands part the air.
They are always just about to arrive.
One woman's asshole fills the room.
One woman's hair is dangerous iron spikes.
Another's nose becomes a blunt stone.
One woman's eyes are broken holes.
Another's eyes bulge like over-ripe fruit.
Some of the shapes try to love one another.
One woman's nostrils unbalance her face.
Another woman's mouth is a short crooked line.
One woman cries stones tied to ropes.
One woman has become a metal house.
Another has become a vase.
Another's head has become an axe head.
One woman weeps light.
Another woman bares her teeth as she weeps.
One woman's hand has become a flower.
A man holding a sheep means to kill it.
One woman's arms are above her head.
Another woman's body is covered in sores.
One woman's shadow watches her float.
Another woman is content to be.

Annual

1. Sky runs down hills. Cedar Waxwings. Rainless days. Silhouette.

2. Elephant Seal howling. I break my head. Yellow pollen mists. Floods.

3. Star-Thistle. Ticks. Vernal pools. Coyotes. Tree tipping. What do I know?

4. Rain. Poppies. Bees drone. No rain. Quail alarm. Rain. Mud. Cornered.

5. Heat. Mosquitoes. Snares. Raven inside. Insomnia. Fumes. I lose my place.

6. Missing days. Tree Frog. Blue Fly. Wildflowers. Gray Fox. I go calling.

7. Fledglings. Gold slope. Water-Spider. Creek sinking. Deer-on-road. Wilt.

8. Dragonflies. Orange dust. Monkey Paw. Heat ripple over empty holes.

9. Orb spiders. Lightning stopping me. Raven stalking meadow.

10. Smudged yellow sky. Cracked-open-ground. I ask for more voices.

11. Rainless warm days. Torrential rain. Swarming Ants. Smoke. Silence.

12. Freezing fog. Chewing wind. Cracked lips. Listening. Traditional omissions.

Song of Ticks

The Dogs are drunk
With Ticks—no matter Twist & Pull
Are Legion & insatiable
Swollen with black stolen blood.

With Ticks—no matter Twist & Pull
Even the Freeze don't kill 'em—
Swollen with black stolen blood.
Ominous black zeppelins

Even the Freeze don't kill 'em—
Like Us, they gorge, remorseless.
Ominous black zeppelins
Like Us, they have no future.

Like Us, they gorge, remorseless.
Cursed by every creature.
Like Us, they have no future.
And my skin crawls, shivers—

Cursed by every creature.
Hunger, but no beloved.
And my skin crawls, shivers—
We can't stop ourselves, we

Hunger, but no beloved.
The Dogs are drunk
We can't stop ourselves, we
Are Legion & insatiable.

Eclogue

"Darkness / is the everlasting verb."
—*Robert Bringhurst*

1. Plow Song

Tractors
Open angry
Ruts—

Today:
The Plowing
Under.

You
Turn starving
Inside out—

Devour Us—

2. The Bait

Fog
Blockading roads
Vineyard—

Valley's
Rippling lights, spiral
Out—

Fool's
Gold, blue
Cloud forms—

House—
Your small red lips—
Delicious!

3. Field Song

Pasture's last hope—
"Mayhap, Mayhap," we sing

To Field's edge—
Weevils, set at thistle's roots

Star Thistle's
Contagion, Bunch Grass left—

"Star's whim, but
Thistle's Hindrance—"

4. Sleep

"Come

Over to my side"
She sings—
But, I cannot.

Windowpane—

Red
Geraniums, Bees
Ding

Windowpane—

Orange mist
In Oaks, Moss
Dripping

And I float

In stone lake
Silence—
"Wake up," She

Sings—

5. Night Planting

Myself, like Maple
Dead asleep—better you
Plant the Bulbs, tuck them
In a muddy hole
Begin waiting—

Corpse light blue Fog
Jeweled Chaparral—

Moon, half sliced away
Rose clouds gone grey—
On my garden slope
Wind scoured away, Leaves
Twigs, Berries, Seed—

6. Cabin Fever

A single Oak holds back the Sun.
Sky, a pulsing gold icon.
The Cabin, a shadow against the dark.
"Please me," said Night, but I could not—

Rat claws inside the wall—
Feverish I sweat this rut you wore
In this wide bed, this stone Cabin
Colder inside than out—
How can we rest?

7. Lullaby

Unscrew—

Pig trough, pink
Worms under
Ice sheet

Unscrew—

Purple
Sky, frozen
Sunflower
Seeds, kibble
Mice cache

Unscrew
In Guest bed
At fold

Nestled—

8. The Music

Giddy fever
Fattens day, each
Moment, wobbly—

"Find music"
Sing Leaves—Is
Shivering dance

Or wheezing
Phrase?—"Find
Music," sing

Leaves—
"These hours
Have teeth—"

I say, "Let
The Dog give
Tongue—"

Sing Leaves

9. Harvest

"Little by little
You'll know—" She says

A Poison here
A Poison there
& we are set to Rally—

Dancing.

Manic Bee
Hums limbs, peers
Black hollows—

"You're to Blame"
She says—

10. The Game

She's plotting—
Wind shoves, the Trees
Just take It—

"Lop the Trees," She says
And I begin to sharpen—
"Don't dither—"

She says
Pulling a circle 'round me—
Everything else

Is Poison—
"Trust Me," She says
As I begin to sharpen—

She's plotting—
Wind shoves, the Trees
Just take It—

11. Sunset

Sunset pins
Us—Ravenous
Bloodletting

We—

Most Natural All.
So the Body describes
I do, I do—

Denial is only love.
The Mouse is in the trap.
"Know your Place—"

I do, I do—

Math

I put 0 and 0 together
And arrived at nothing.
Nothing was accomplished.
I had done it perfectly.
I made 0 disappear into 0.
I made sure nothing was left.
There was no doubt of it.

Next, I made 2 into two.
It was easy: numbers are words.
I made sure nothing was left.
I made sure nothing was said.
I made sure nothing was written.
It was getting complicated.

My thumb was black with ink.
So, everything I touched became
Itself plus me.
Every addition complicated it.
Every mark was a number.
Every number mocked.

I settled on the number one.
I refused all manner of addition.
I was careful to touch nothing.
"That's impossible," someone said.
I knew someone was right.

The Trouble with You

Moss, Grass crackle in hand.
Leaf, Root, Flower, Fruit, orders Garden.
"The trouble with you," she says—
& I'm a ladder left leaning on a Tree.

Leaf, Root, Flower, Fruit, orders Garden.
Frost puts to slumber, sleep . . .
& I'm a ladder left leaning on a Tree.
Put on some Music & we'll pretend—

Frost puts to slumber, sleep . . .
Snow Berry stars in an empty Wood.
Put on some Music & we'll pretend—
Blood-stained box the Turkey rode in.

Snow Berry stars in an empty Wood.
I can't look you in the eye, just how we are
Blood-stained box the Turkey rode in.
Nothing older or more terrible—

I can't look you in the eye, just how we are
Last Leaves, yellow mobiles, smile, smile
Nothing older or more terrible—
Put on some Music & we'll pretend—

Last Leaves, yellow mobiles, smile, smile
Moss & Grass crackle in hand.
Put on some Music & we'll pretend—
"The trouble with you," she says—

Him

"Words are tools," She said
& broke the spell, set me free—
Quail sang, Rattlesnake sang

"His gifts will eat you," She said
So I took nothing with me, only
Hunger, I was very hungry—

"Trick Him with sleep," She said
So I sang to Him like Cricket
As I nailed Him to his shadow—

"Don't pity Him," She said
So I knew it was my weakness
When at dawn He slipped away—

He grew impossible to follow.
"Everyone has their shadow," She said—
His was mine.

III

"I am not empty, I am open."

—*Tomas Tranströmer*

Triage

I arrive early
Before the Others
Are done speaking

While the doors
Are shut before
Newcomers arrive

Waiting to speak.
I arrive early. While
The doors are shut

Words escape me
When the doors open.
I am alone.

Waiting to speak.
I shut the doors softly.
Words escape.

Fable

—for Esther Traugot

1.

I began innocently enough
Dressing the Apple tree in unmatched socks
To dissuade the Deer from grazing
To deter the Codling Moths from burrowing
To keep the Squirrels at bay—
After all, the fruit was mine.

2.

Socks made Tree's limbs look naked.
What if I clothed them too, used hooks & yarn?
I decided to crochet in gold.
Twigs too delicate for yarn, I stitched with string
Disguising every seam with tiny knots.
I gilded Tree, limb by limb—
Black twig tips I left unclothed, so light
And wind might fondle them.

3.

I couldn't stop stitching.
Seashell was empty, its silence lost
To echoes, exiled to noise.
What could I do but fill it? Go at it
With hooks & yarn. If a living Tree
Could be clothed, why not a Shell?
In Shell's blue spiral, I nested gold squares.
Shell was luminous, silent again.

4.

Then, oblong, unbalanced Egg
Fragile, alone, needed to be clothed.
I hooked a hood of thin gold thread.
I left a pale oval, where a face
Might appear. I never dropped a stitch.
My hooks sang only being or nothingness.
Egg pulsed gold light—
Its dark inside secure.

5.

Where my yarn lapsed, shadows
Began, extending every object out in time.
Fine gradated shadows of the Apples
The Tree, the Shell, the Egg—
Shadows articulating time, its
Ceaseless touching, prodding on.
There was no way to intervene, to save.
My hands lay folded in my lap.
The gold quivering with light.

Song for Oyster

Harvesters—

Foreheads aglow
Follow the tide to Oyster.
Sea recedes, mud flats

Oyster beds—
Charcoal black rows
Of ropes & stakes—

Pry him loose.
Shuck him Out—
Eat him alive.

Living for Others

As I came to life
The human Swarm devoured—
Just a drone, I dissolved
Into the pulse of the Hive.

I'm doing what I can
White days, alone—
To keep the Barn Cat eating
And the bent house leaning—
Trying not to think ahead
While the inconvenient Plants are dying.

Song for Dying

—for John Powell
  (1965–2004)

It's a race to bottom
Raven pecks a dead Possum
Cat licks rain off the Hosta—

but John who put Death in
topper & buckled shoes is dead
dead, dead—

Ants milk Aphid flocks
their sticky honeydew—I was
the Maypole, the Maypole—

as Cottonwoods loose white
seed clouds, I'm in a gypsy
wagon with you

but John who put Death in
topper & buckled shoes is dead
dead, dead—

"Picture's not dark, it's Dark
Woods," he said, "Stinging Nettles
are best," he said, said

John who put Death in
topper & buckled shoes is dead
dead, Dead—

The Hare
—*after Beuys*

Once harm is done
Does art overcome
A dead Hare?

First spring grass
Already browning, where
Am I to go?

Every action I take
Increases my suffering—
Have you no advice?

Contest

I go to the gallery.
The pictures stare at me.

Even their lips stare.
Long as they stare, I stare back.

They always win.
They're experts at desire.

Their hands are Spiders.
They use their hands to conceal.

I let lines form between our eyes
As their bodies sponge up light—

I float in my watery body.

Unspoken

He sees me—
He's underfoot
Rustles grass:

Forked tongue
Sniffs Gopher holes—

And I'm in my skin.
I watch my step.
I say nothing

As a couple embraces
On the grass.

Upstairs

—for Robert Lowell

All day the workmen bang & stomp
knocking the windows out
fitting the new, uglier windows in
piling the old ones, like broken spectacles
against the Tree, their slow glass
rippling the bark & leaves
torn bits of rope & counterweights
tossed on the porch—

then, the vacuuming begins
& next the carpet sweeper
everything must be moved to clean
behind & under & squeak & stomp go on
'til the Sun sets & the dark flows
evenly from room to room
from room to garden—
then it is safe to sleep
to stop thinking about loss.

Counting the Animals

Ten Pelicans, one interloping Gull
Ride thermals up granite cliffs, northmost-point
McClure's Beach.

Ten female Elk, face out, vigilant
Along the ridgeline, mist overtaking them
And the bony Bishop Pines.

Ten Cormorants, one Pelican
Motionless on black-rock-island. Behind them
In a rookery in the cliff, birds

Uncounted.

Washroom (Oil Spill)

I hold Cormorant
As gently as I can—
I must control her head

I must exert pressure
(how much pressure?)
On her neck—

Brown foam slathers
Her—Iridescent heaving
As she Panics—

We slow, to help
Her catch her breath.
Then, we begin again—

Tanka

Blue-eyed Cormorant
I hold to feed, medicate—
Plunges head under
Unzips my arm, wobbles me—
Bloodied animal I am.

Memorandum of Birds

—On Rauschenberg

Below Bird's Wing
Is a Hazard of Circles—

Why is Rooster
Perched on an Odalisque?

Why is a Rooster
Striding, Paint-bedecked?—

Black Block Letters
Tumble out of the Sky—

Wings, stiff with Paint
Are wired down—

An Inlet is an Egret
In a box, Revolver

& Compass, provided—

Eclipse

This evening eclipse
Perplexes me, as if the day
Had got ahead of itself
By stumbling
On some forgotten obstacle—
Pitched forward
As though plush darkness
Was just ahead to cushion
Its fall, to let it down easy.
Leaves' shadows are rent
To sickle-shaped remnants
Fingers' shadows whittled
Away, it's dimming, cooling
Birds gone, dusk chorus
Skipped—
Then, at the last instant
Day catches itself, rights itself:
A slow seesaw rebuttal
Dark retreats, shadows
Flip, cast their opposites
And that golden hour, before
Twilight is restored, must be
Lived all over again. The chorus
Begins.

Diary

I feel Cat. Cat feels me. There is no need to say "I am here," for we are Here; there is no need to say "I think," because we both Feel. Cat and I are Feeling Here and being Here with each other. Cherry Tree is Here, Feeling alongside us and Magnolia and Climbing Rose, all Feeling the Yellow beyond the Poplars, Feeling the Rain that is to follow.

Feeling is older than words, it is language of World. It does not exclude, it includes all and every; it does not change, it is Change itself, a Lake we are already swimming in, Air that is already in our lungs and around our bodies. The language of Feeling needs nothing of the language of words. The language of words is the language of consumption, not the language of Power.

Feeling is the language of Power; the Power of the body of the World, to speak to itself. The World is not a thing—the World is not an action or thing, it is a living Being made up of living Beings. Our bodies are not things, they are living Beings made of living Beings, all in the conversation of Feeling. The World must speak to itself, it must Feel itself, its organs and their Being, like I feel my fingers typing, like I feel my stomach is empty.

Our bodies are always inside and outside. But there is not Cat and I—only the Feeling we share. My body is many bodies, many Creatures I carry. I Feel my body, I Feel with my body. Every body inside every body, outside every body, speaks with Feeling. Words are not Feelings, words are not bodies; they are nouns or verbs. Feeling is Body, the Body is the World, the Body we inhabit and the Bodies that inhabit us. Only Words or Death can separate a Body from itself—separate a Body from Feeling.

Words are not Feeling. To Feel is to Join; words do not Join, words separate. Feelings do not separate, they Join. There is no way to make words Feel another, words only say themselves. The language of Feeling Feels itself as part of the Feeling of Being, but the Feeling of Being is not a noun or a verb, it is both. There is no word for the Feeling of Being, for Joining. Language is not Joining, it is one speaker, one speaker at a time. Being is not one being at a time, Being is World.

I do not speak to the Maple, because the Maple is not a word. I Feel the Maple, for it is a Body and my hands wave like Leaves. When the Chestnut drops its glossy Seed, I do not praise it with words, I take its Seed and eat it and the Chestnut I and Join in the Feeling of autumn rains and the moist greenness of Being. The Chestnut is the language of Feeling. I am not the Chestnut, but I am the language of Feeling. We are not one and the other; there is no addition or subtraction, only Life and the life within our life and the Lives that include us.

Familiar

You comfort me
Make dark into a den:
Breath circulates

Our bodies warm—

My name melts:
Only we are here—
We are unafraid

We curl into sleep:
Your spine & mine
Our vertebrae fuse—

We travel on as one.

Golden Book

—*from* The Golden Book, *1917*

morning	sun	rises	hills
glad	here	are	awaken

The night is done.

The day is here.

I awaken when it is day.

The flowers awaken when it is day.

I see the sun in the sky.

The sun rises above the hills.

The sun rises above the trees.

The birds and flowers are glad to see the sun.

Are you glad the night is done?

Haiku

Hurrying in rain

I lift a Snail from the path—

Where are you going?

IV

"... man does not consist only of chemical processes, but also of metaphysical occurrences."

—Joseph Beuys

Utopia Parkway

It's easy to see
how we forget ourselves

in the rain's momentary
colonnades & passageways:

things are not
as they could be; the animal

is cold, tired, hungry
& every question is a question

of human nature, a warmth
that clings to the sheets, whims

& dreams intertwined—
"fold up absolutely flat

& then unfold into stars."

2.

Even a forest knit to a hill
passes between worlds—

(a "deer's foot imprinted
in mint bed") releases

a trace & melts away, a trace
trembles the air &

I am awake, all things being
equal, a blade of grass

equal to the suffering
of a lifetime, a passing away

into things "wagons
& vehicles in motion,

vehicles of fantasy—"

3.

"This benedictory beauty
'the American scene'"

backyard rustic antics
the old dog's nose to the wind

"to 'catch it' (being) life"—
stars in the leaves over the house

soap-bubble constellations
(light years ago)

& what is to be done
even before we spoke

all still to be done.

4.

Under the house, things
take on a life of their own

dirt keeps finding its way in
& nothing will stay put—

house & darkness fuse
"something quiet working

out from 'nothing'"—
time rising up out of things

like steam rising off the fence—

the old dog licks my hand
to keep walking

unseen hands guide me
"Orion wheeling towards

the horizon," invisible dark
feeding life & its light

sustaining it—

5.

Wandering room-to-room, dematerializing—

these lessons in my body, sugary high words
then exhaustion

& the dream of a blue peninsula, so purposefully quiet
& hard to find—

"the ineffable—its warmth & freshness"
is nothing like I imagined:

a gray squirrel rolling in dirt, dusting up
the light.

6.

"The wonder of light
especially 'life continuing'"

giggles, freckles & the blush of youth—

a slip of a girl, hips & shoulders
asway, all the green spring leaves

drinking up the light—

how did I become so sure
watching the fence rot away

visible & invisibles

the scent of pine needles
& fresh cut grass—

this immense stillness
to which I can add nothing

like some "elation of star gazing"
joining us in & of itself

like wind caressing the grass

like something sweet
we lick off our fingertips.

7.

A young buck (his horns
fleshy stubs) rears up

on the green clipped lawn
(belly flashing white)

stealing apples, licking
the juice from his dark lips—

all our "flashing & yearning"
like swallows, diving

into our own darkness, "again
beautiful & unfailing,"—

the crows are adamant
the god-like trees are theirs

& theirs—
& the fear that drove us

mad with death & treachery
that, "(should not even

be spoken of)"

8.

One "half struck down
one half still bearing blossoms—"

I try to make myself appear
"where the 'blue swallow'

(the dark one) was last seen"
where a fly with one wing keeps

tipping over in the grass, where
the ants will have him

where all that's done is done—
The blackbirds wake me

sing me to sleep, back "into
those dreams of woods

relayed to you"—

ACKNOWLEDGMENTS

To my editor, Mark Levine, my profound gratitude for his generous contributions and creative engagement.

My thanks to the editors of the journals in which these poems first appeared: "Nest" and "Upstairs" appeared in *American Poetry Review*; "Living for Others" appeared in *Canary*; "Dream (I dream a reactor . . .)" appeared in *The Fulcrum: a magazine of ammunition*; "Song of Ticks" appeared in *The Iowa Review*; "Utopia Parkway" appeared in *The Jung Journal: Culture & Psyche*; "Tanka," "Walk," and "Washroom (Oil Spill)" appeared in *Poetry Flash*; "The Trouble with You" appeared in *Unsplendid*; "A Natural History" appeared in *The West Marin Review*. "Familiar" appeared as a Pocket Poem in the April 2014 series published by Mrs. Dalloway's bookstore in Berkeley, California.

To Esther Traugot, Samuel Charters, Robert Bringhurst, Kate Donahue, Allison DeLauer, Ned Balbo, Jane Satterfield, Kate Colby, Monte Merrick, Laura Corsiglia, John Laskey, Ekaterina Taratuta, Laura Olson, James Vincent Colbert, Tedd Siegel, Marc Romano, Jens Hillmer, and Henry Epstein, my heartfelt appreciation for their invaluable support.

NOTES

Page 1.   John Baptiste (translator), "Wakdjunkaga," in Paul Radin, Winnebago Notebooks, Freeman #3897 (Philadelphia: American Philosophical Society, ca. 1912) Winnebago V, #7: 567–568. Used with permission of the copyright holder, American Philosophical Society.

Page 10.   "Stalker" references the film *Stalker,* dir. Andrei Tarkovsky, Mosfilm, 1979.

Page 11.   "Passport" is for David Abram.

Page 12.   "The Inquisitor" as well as "Song of Ticks" and "The Trouble with You" follow John Ashbery's variation on the pantoum, which appeared in his book *Some Trees.*

Page 19.   John Berryman, "Dream Song 352," *The Dream Songs* (New York: Farrar, Straus and Giroux, 1969), 374. Used with permission of the copyright holder, Kate Donahue.

Page 28.   "Annual" is formally inspired by Native American Calendar texts in Leona Cope, "North American Calendar Lists," *Io/6*, Ethnoastronomy Issue (Summer 1969): 166–167.

Page 30.   Robert Bringhurst, "Pythagoras," *Selected Poems* (London: Jonathan Cape, 2010), 30. Used with permission of the copyright holder, Robert Bringhurst.

Page 45.   Tomas Tranströmer, "Vermeer," *Tomas Tranströmer: Selected Poems 1954–1986*, ed. Robert Hass (New York: The Ecco Press, 1987), 187. Used with permission of the translator and copyright holder, Samuel Charters.

Page 48.   "Fable" was written for a reading accompanying an exhibition featuring the work of Esther Traugot at the Chandra Cerrito Contemporary gallery in Oakland, California, on July 14, 2012.

Page 51.   "Living for Others" was Philip Larkin's working title for his collection *High Windows.*

Page 53.   "The Hare" references an "Action" by Joseph Beuys titled "How to Explain Pictures to a Dead Hare," undertaken in Düsseldorf on November 26, 1965 at Galerie Schmela.

Page 58.   The oil spill is the 2007 Cosco Busan spill in San Francisco Bay. The poem is for Monte Merrick.

Page 62.   "Diary" is formally informed by *The Diary of Vaslav Nijinsky: Unexpurgated Edition*, ed. Joan Acocella (New York: Farrar, Straus and Giroux, 1999).

Page 65.   "Golden Book" is a found poem. *The Golden Book*, ed. Reverend Newton Marshall Hall and Reverend Irving Francis Wood (Springfield: 1917), 44.

Page 67.   *Energy Plan for the Western Man: Joseph Beuys in America*, ed. Carin Kuoni (New York: Four Walls Eight Windows, 1990), 87. Used with permission, ©2014 Artists Rights Society (ARS), New York / VG Bild-Kunst, Bonn.

Pages 69–76. Quotations "extended" in "Utopia Parkway" are from *Joseph Cornell's Theater of the Mind: Selected Diaries, Letters, and Files*, ed. Mary Ann Caws (New York: Thames and Hudson, 1993).

KUHL HOUSE POETS

Christopher Bolin
Ascension Theory

Shane Book
Congotronic

Oni Buchanan
Must a Violence

Michele Glazer
On Tact, & the Made Up World

David Micah Greenberg
Planned Solstice

Jeff Griffin
Lost and

John Isles
Ark

John Isles
Inverse Sky

Randall Potts
Trickster

Bin Ramke
Airs, Waters, Places

Bin Ramke
Matter

Michelle Robinson
The Life of a Hunter

Robyn Schiff
Revolver

Robyn Schiff
Worth

Rod Smith
Deed

Cole Swensen
The Book of a Hundred Hands

Cole Swensen
Such Rich Hour

Tony Tost
Complex Sleep

Susan Wheeler
Meme

Emily Wilson
The Keep